MARKHAM COLLEGE

STUDIIS ET REBUS HONESTIS

PRESENTED
TO

JEFFREY LOTTERMAN

FOR

PROGRESS AND EFFORT – Grade 2U

1981

Acknowledgements

Heather Angel 8 bottom left, 39 bottom, 44 top; W. B. Baker 20 top; Barnaby's Picture Library 8–9; John Bethell 34–35; S. C. Bisserot 10 bottom, 44 bottom; J. Allan Cash 27; Bruce Coleman: Jane Burton 36, 38 top; W. F. Davidson 4 top, 12 bottom, 14 inset, 18 top and bottom, 20 bottom, 23 top, 40 inset, 42, 43 top; Adrian Davies 37 top, 38 bottom; Brian Hawkes 9, 45 inset; David Hosking 15; Roger Hosking front cover; E. A. Janes front and back endpapers, 4 bottom, 6, 7 bottom, 22, 25 bottom, 39 top; Natural History Photographic Agency: Anthony Bannister 17 top, Joe Blossom 21, Stephen Dalton 7 top, 10 top, J. B. Free 30–31, Walter Murray 8 bottom right, L. E. Perkins 17 bottom, James Tallon 30; Natural Science Photos: Noel McFarland 32 bottom, C. Mattison 32 top, Mark Stanley Price 33; Seaphot: Walter Deas 41, 43 bottom, Bill Howes 37 bottom; David Sewell 45; Spectrum Colour Library 35; Tony Stone Associates 11, 12 top, 14–15, 16 top and bottom, 19, 23 bottom, 29, 40–41, back cover; ZEFA: P. W. Bading 28, Danim 29 inset, W. F. Davidson 26, W. Harstrick 13, W. Kratz 25 top, G. Mabbs 24, Hans Reinhard 5.

Other books in the series:
People of the World
Things that Move
Young Animals

Published 1979 by
The Hamlyn Publishing Group Limited
London · New York · Sydney · Toronto
Astronaut House, Feltham, Middlesex, England

ISBN 0 600 36338 4

Printed and bound by Group Poligrafici Calderara, Bologna, Italy -

Hamlyn First Colour Books

Nature

Hamlyn
London · New York · Sydney · Toronto

In summer the weather
is warm.
Then there are lots of
colourful flowers.
Insects like the summer.
This butterfly is feeding
from a flower.
He is sucking up some
sweet liquid that the
flower produces.
Here is a grass snake.
He likes to come out
and lie in the warm sun.
A grass snake is
harmless but some
snakes are poisonous.

You can look at nature
in the garden.
There are lots of
different plants and
creatures there.
Birds often make their
nests in a garden.
Here is a linnet finishing
her nest.
This thrush's children
have already hatched.
Can you see what she
has for them to eat?
This hoverfly is having a
meal too.

This garden dormouse is in an apple tree.
He sleeps all winter.
In summer he likes to eat fruit.
These red creatures are ladybirds.
Their favourite food is greenfly.
Do you think there are enough here for a meal?

Here is a field of corn.
Sometimes you may see
red flowers like this one
growing in the field.
It is a poppy.
Corn has flowers too.
There are different sorts
of corn.
This sort of corn is rye.
Can you see its flowers?

Trees are the largest
plants in the world.
All these trees are in a
wood.
Some leaves have
turned brown and have
fallen off.
Can you tell what
season it is?
Lots of creatures live in
the wood.
Here is a woodpecker.
She has a long strong
beak for pecking insects
off the tree.

Here is a weasel.
He is watching
something in the wood.
These badgers live in
the wood.
They only come out of
their homes at night.
What a large beetle!
It is a stag beetle.
He is not as fierce as he
looks.
Where can all these ants
be going?
They are looking for
something to eat.

A lot of different plants
grow in the wood.
These yellow flowers
are primroses.
Here are two fir-cones.
They are growing on a
spruce tree and have
seeds inside them.
You can often see
toadstools in the wood.
They look pretty but
they are poisonous.
This vole lives in the
wood.
He is not eating the
toadstools.

This black creature is a mole.
He is very good at digging, as he makes his home underground.
The red clover grows in the field above the mole's home.
There is a deer in the field too.
Can you see what he likes to eat?

Can you see all the different seeds here?
There are seeds growing inside the red berries.
Birds like to eat the berries.
They will drop the seeds, which will begin to grow.
These acorns will fall off the tree when they are
ready and will grow into more oak trees.
The seeds of a dandelion are very light.
The wind will blow them away.

In spring, things begin to grow.
Flowers grow on the tree before there are apples.
These flowers turn into fruit.
Here is the beginning of a beech tree.
Can you imagine how it can grow into a big tree?
These crocuses are having to grow in the snow.
Can you see them peeping through?

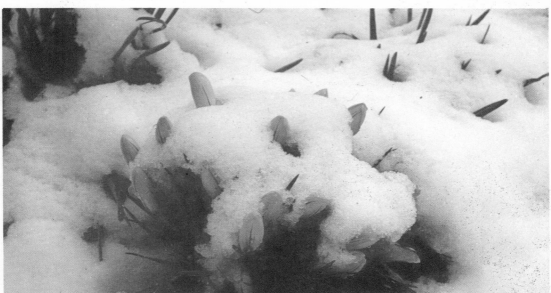

Winter is the coldest season of the year.
In some places there is lots of snow in winter.
Most trees lose all their leaves.
Animals grow thicker coats in the winter.
Some animals can change the colour of their coats.
This hare has some white fur to match the snow.
It helps him to hide when he is in danger.

Some animals like polar bears live in snow all the
year round.
Here is one on the ice in Alaska.
He has a very thick coat.
These wolves are happy playing in the snow.
The snow round this deer is very deep.
Do you think he has fallen over?
He even has snow on the top of his head.

Certain parts of the
world are very dry.
They are deserts.
Only a few plants can
live there.
These palm trees have
very shiny leaves.
They do not lose too
much water in the sun.
A cactus can survive for
a long time in the desert.
It stores water.
This one is a funny
shape.

Not many animals can live in the desert.
This herd of camels can live without water for
some time.
Men use them for crossing the desert.
There are lots of different lizards in the world.
Some like these can live in very dry lands.
These two lizards are very different.
Which one do you think is most handsome?

Some animals live in or
near water.
There is salt water and
fresh water.
Rivers and ponds are
fresh water.
Can you think what
animals live by this
river?
The kingfisher likes to
live near the river.
He catches small fish.
This kingfisher has
caught one.
Can you see it?

These otters have made their home by the river.
They love to swim and splash in the water.
Fish swim in the river too.
Here is a trout.
He must be careful when the otters are near.
A trout is an otter's favourite food.
This beautiful dragonfly frightens smaller insects.
He can catch them as they fly past.

You can see many animals and plants in a pond.
These tadpoles will soon grow into frogs.
Some snails also live under the water.
Waterlillies float on top of the water.
They close their petals at night.
Can you see the bulrushes growing?

The seashore is full of
animals and plants.
Lots of them live on the
beach.
There are animals under
the water too.
Some of them are very
strange but they are
very pretty.
Here is a sea-star.
Do you think you can
count all the arms?
The sea-urchin is very
prickly.
The prickles are really
arms too.

Here are some different sorts of seaweed that grow
on the beach.
Some of them need lots of water, but some only
need a little.
The turtle has come out of the sea to lay her eggs.
You might see a crab like this on the beach.

A lobster has very
powerful claws.
This little yellow creature
is called a seahorse.
He is really a fish.
These gannets like to live
in large groups.
Can you see the young
one?
It is fun to watch nature.
Did you know any of the
things in this book?